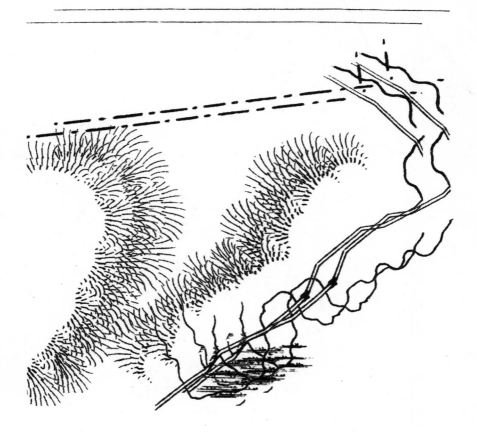

Maps for Jackie

JASON LABBE

BLAZEVOX[BOOKS]
Buffalo, New York

publisher of weird little books

BlazeVOX [books]

blazevox.org

21 20 19 18 17 16 15 14 13 12 01 02 03 04 05 06 07 08 09 10

BlazeVOX

Contents

Great Circle Distance

The Valley

Postcards from the Periphery

Maps for Jackie

Where have I gone, Beloved?

Into the Wlatz, Dancer.

—Robert Duncan

Great Circle Distance

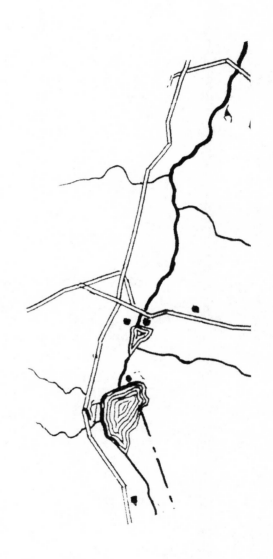

Map of the Ferns

All my unsent letters begin in a way
part elegy, part epistle—
a map of grief in the second person.

But this approach isn't direct enough,
the patch of ferns too broad, wilting
between two stands of pine.

In all my letters the point is lost
to innuendo. Each frond withers frail
under summer. In all my letters

the question still blinks but never
fully comes on, like the shorting streetlight
beyond that filthy bedroom window

years ago, Manhattan Avenue: on, off, on...
In that apartment you couldn't see
past my glaring poverty, and the question

flashed, street-level and drafty
when January took over. A decade later,
mid-July, there are no more letters.

But the question still nags, asking and asking
as I walk along the Housatonic.
Do you believe there is a place for us?

My right steps say we belong in the ferns.
My last left step says
we belong in the middle of the river.

Lullaby for Jackie

I was downed in your daring, Jackie,
I wouldn't dodge what you deserved,
and didn't, was yours, spun out and slid

into that oak, damp with drizzle, I was
a drop, I *dropped*, adorned
your deployment of black smoke,

two lanes and no shoulder, four flat tires,
a fire of them, *darling*, indifferent,
and so ambivalent we didn't

sleep until December, you insisted
you needn't, such dependence, never drowsy
enough, *it* was indispensable, and so I said

with involuntary gestures to the white
coat behind the counter, *honey hurry*,
I was dust, not dusty, hardly managed

to drive myself, in spite of mild sun,
said *sweetheart*, pick me up, *baby* don't,
and never so raw as dawn

did we defend our need to the doctors,
who just left me standing there, a degree
of abandonment, and I was ashamed in saying

don't look at me, *sugar*, unless the dream
of sunrise that taunts from the window dissipates.
Jackie, don't be here come morning.

Aubade

Waking finds
morning the inmost warp
in spacetime—

I host from the distance
I need to recognize
you ghosting

my chest cavity.
I don't need a bottle
bedside to tell me: *empty.*

A mountain: one slice of
dry toast, two cups of black tea.
To chase a truer seam

between rock and stream—
unaccompanied—
demanded abandoning

your colder ocean.

Map of the BLUE BLUE BLUE

I have a blue sliver of hot aluminum.
I have a hot blue sliver in my middle finger.
Just below my knuckle I have a flash
of blue glinting as though the weather
were fairer than the fluorescent light
of my basement, warmer than the terrible
voice mail I have informing me
of the latest sighting. You're back in town
and your drunken face is all sunken in.
I have a sister who warns me of you.
I love my sister who hates the smell
of your lies and thieving as much as I do.
I have taken a year to take inventory.
What I have left I have bolted to the floor,
except this sliver of blue aluminum infecting
my middle finger. I have a workshop
in my basement and a father who taught me
how to design, fabricate, and assemble
a precision machine. I cut and mill
and turn and drill. Soon I will complete
the Blue Machine to protect us from you.
My middle finger finesses my micrometer,
it adjusts the tooling when the dimensions
from the blue print slip out of tolerance.
My middle finger is primary as the sliver
and grows bluer because I strangle it
with a silvery blue ribbon, all nice and curled

at its ends. Here, have it and keep it
forever. The rest, everything else you see,
is for me. But my blue, it gleams for you.

Map of Every Residential Neighborhood

Chase me down
after the dark turn
every late party is bound

to take. Keep your eye
on my rusting
tailgate as I hit

ninety in a twenty-five.
Let all the careless things
I said by the bonfire

spin in your head
and weigh on
your gas pedal.

If I overshoot the hairpin
be the one
to call my wife

at dawn. Tell her
not about the tree, or the twist
of metal, rubber, glass—

Confess everything
about you and me:
cold sunrise, black branches.

My Polar Bear

My hair was black as hers
before it was as white. Afternoon

echoed in the blowsy meadow
as she led
our deadly waltz under the willow.

When I was thirsty she offered the stream
that fed the lake. Salt on a finger.

She grabbed the wheel,
and out the window I swore
the white trees were running. Two winters

dragged. She entered the instant
I turned my back to the deadbolted door.

In the aerospace factory she turned
the handwheel of my lathe.
I kept a finger on the feed dial
and we doubled
the quota of aluminum fuel nozzles.

All the jets overhead flew faster
with her face in every window.

Evenings her dreadnought stayed in tune
I dreamt of a bullet stalling in midair.
One humid night
the strings went slack and she fell

flat. Dragged the tempo, forgot
the words.
I had to clean and load my rifle.

I keep her dewclaw in my lip.

Map of Primary Colors

In the dark her walls were red.
She was talking into my mouth, a thread
not of words but pure vibration.

Her thin finger traced the stitching,
her thin finger pinned me to the bed,
her thin finger said, Listen close

to the clouds, listen to the clouds close.
Rain leaking through the skylight dripped
into the bowl she carved from driftwood.

In the dark mirror, two silhouettes,
then one. She called this game Evening
and my silence was her only rule—

she was talking into my mouth
to lift my dread of nothing to say.
In the red I found the reason

her pincushion resembles a tomato
which resembles a heart. Her tongue
needled my nerves. *This is her bed.*

The thread frayed as I followed it
and Evening gave way to yellow:
broken yolks, scraps of fabric, sun

through the sun of a stained glass window.
I wanted to hear my name again—
her call that once led my winter bird

across a county of hard rain faded,
an echo in the bright corners.
I followed Morning's two rules—stay,

leave—and the crack in the skylight
flashed across an open view.
In the light her walls were blue.

Apology as Map of the Illegible

Summer's finale
is a glass of ice, early pear
on the lowest branch

not yet bending down

to instruct where
to begin, again belatedly
in cursive and imperfect

A bat darts between trees
Its path is jagged
erratic across

blue going black
No moths collect by the dead
flood light

Nightfall suspends
the droning motors in the distance
We trail off

And something else curves

toward the red
couch on the flaking grey
porch of nobody's repose

A nerve in the hand which gestures
what can't be read
pressures the point

Summer wears off

What shouldn't have been said
now almost melted
almost illegible
Night will hang
rangy and frayed overhead
until the heat lets up

up and you

Great Circle Distance

Can you shrug off
the debt, the theft, the elapsing
threat and the worry

that keeps you
pacing and sleepless.
What you don't want

you want to rationalize.
Does a line by hand
have to *waver* across

the imagined map, angle
of afternoon shifting
imperceptibly across dust

on the floor. What's with you,
hard on the eyes
in this light. If it's too cold

to close the window
you are too close.
The thought occurs

but only the thought
of tracing a cinematic horizon
before brushing sundown's blur

of trees, going so late so fast
the edges of the road quiver.
But it's too light, still,

for eyes in the grass. Grainy
in the frame: not the snowy side
of the branch, beak

to bare ground at daybreak,
but swamp and rust
beyond the cartography.

The daydream of
heat leads
the whole body shivering

and you pause
at the boundary—
hour, doorway, traffic light—

Jackie.
Skid to a stop
with the kind of edgy jerk

that would embarrass
a passenger. If you had one,
if you left.

Winter fails to insulate
your window from the drone
of rigs on the interstate.

But if the route's audible
it's not impossible, a nano-
meter wide between

a shriek and a breath,
either a wave into ether.
The rugged stretch to Jackie,

camped somewhere between
Devil's Tower and Death Valley,
is not exactly stationary—

Any ground lost is gained,
every range and desert
contracting and expanding.

Viking Funeral for Jackie

I don't have your best interest anywhere
near the still sunken portion of my chest.
Unless ruined, and so overrated, you fester.

If it's not impossible you're uninterested.
What vestige of our resting will be
sequestered, in which world will the restless

never have to face you, nevertheless
recognize the only way one can walk away.
Every breath is our last, every lament.

            *

The future most unlikely is the one most
imagined—nobody here but us, crystalline,
a constellation. The pines around the lake

soft and black, night sky, the scrape
of the ropes tightening after I lay your body
on the pyre. And mine over yours.

Slowly the fire catches at our feet.
The lake is almost an oval and has one
visible side—no moon shines inside the water

warming, teeming, unrippling. But there
is light. What unseen other shoves us off,
what void fails to be our final thought.

Daguerreotypes of Jackie

What's the difference between a confederate flag
and a broken window? Bring a thermos of coffee and we'll walk
the battlefield. What new amalgam of dusk light, eyeshine,
and dismemberment can be captured in a glass plate
negative, how long must we stage the landscape
before we know in the present moment what to salvage
as artifact? The answer to a handful of riddles:
artifacts have no present moment. I know of no society
which values a scar across the abdomen more than money,
but I have dreamed a greenhouse of repurposed plates
from which I watch your form in the bloody grass emerge.
Marching drums approach. We hum nothing of retreat.

*

What's the difference between a quest and a journey?
If the gate to the field is locked

and we jump it, if the humidity
gets inside us before midnight, then show me the stone
I'll threaten to throw through the visitor center window.
The *stone* is a buzzing phone in your jacket pocket.
Say *don't*. Say my name, Virginia. Call me
Dead Eye—even if I could stop myself I wouldn't.
In the middle of all this galloping, centuries of it,
spread our blanket. In the echo of hooves, only the soil
and the ghost of us. Animal body,

moth breath, your hand is freezing.

*

Which answer leads to fewer questions about the origin?—
of my leaving, of our wanting, or whether your/my hand
is ever warm enough. I was born in a northern valley

where any crumbling brass mill not yet demolished
nobody dreams. We ask about *history* and *nightfall*
to hear a familiar phrase come down the tracks

in the breaking hour. Blood in the grass dries outside
the hour, outside the battle of its cause, but not outside
the range of your voice calling as a coal train beyond

the battlefield. With your thumb, retrace the Mason Dixon,
my surgical scar. Ask where I learned to swear like that.
Let me pretend you don't know. The hour is breaking.

*

What's the difference between a secret and a mystery?
Over my valley, five states north, a V of geese points
toward a fieldstone wall, the distinction between *backwards*
and *reversal.* Because brightness is a symptom
of certain absence, I borrowed this explanation of solstice
from iodine fumes and a lateral sense of this field, diminishing
memory of my light-filled room. Who could stand
sitting so still so long, in midday sun, in her best dress.
To arrive in Virginia in terribly fragile condition.
We *never.* We drag a stick along the perimeter, we bask
in nightfall—this waking dusk made of grass
made of blood. Once the light knows you I won't.

*

Is white supremacy the dark or
Mason Dixon, vague distinction. Will you forgive me

if I mistake the absence of light
for the absence of color? Everything was a gross yellow

until I broke the floodlight with your flip phone.
I can throw a fit and still nail my target.

My heart is a thermal collector is a sick joke
and you know I don't want to hear you fake

knowledge of the supposed science of heartbreak.
If physical matter is infinitely subdividable, then

infinitesimal light enters each point of contact.
Hold the warm hand that I love to my throat.

*

Why did the Union soldier cross the road?
                            If I interrupt your anecdote
about some long-ago boy's finger in your mouth
to piss behind a tree, will I lose you, would you even take me
back from the shroud of night sounds and shadow.
Overhead a jet crescendos then decrescendos
and there are no crickets for a minute.

                            Talk me back, then hold my breath
for another twelve seconds so our faces assume
a level of detail that, like the wings tattooed across my chest,
can't be known in morning light. We relive
                            where the Blue Ridge Mountains begin.

*

What's the distance between a question and its answer?
Spell of cloud cover—moon gone for a minute prolongs exposure
and lengthens the expanse between my valley of cinderblocks and cigarettes

and your Idaho of I don't know. I have drawn a map
of my vulgarity. Trace the valley with an icy finger, walk
across my back. The hour breaks like a rib. How do we separate

without injury, how do I leave us
without blood in the grass getting in your hair. Must I
remind you that none of this is fair or easy—a felled tree

lies at the edge of the battlefield until it becomes a raccoon
and an exploding planet. Unrequited we shall orbit
the raccoon from a tropical planet beyond the exploding planet.

*

How many amputee ghosts does it take to defeat terrorism?
Asking me to tell you the battlefield's history, about
dawn, is asking me to say

                 Jackie. Lead me across the breaking hour
      as though we could even *think* of sleeping
      without the sound of birds.
      Why should we
when we can go so much lower with everything else peeking up.
Saying each other's names breaks the minutes
before sunrise, before sleep. I cannot silence these questions.
How do I release myself from the valley of bleeding knuckles
or hold your breath for another twelve seconds.

The Valley

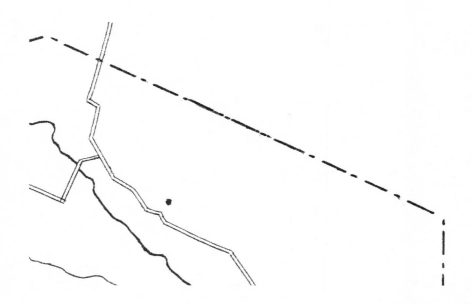

Map of May 20

My frontal lobe roams the lowest
forest of the Valley. The door
almost opened itself. I blame the white

stone hidden deep in my inside
pocket, though my jacket's in tatters,
unwearable, left on the floor

of somewhere I don't want to live anymore.
The hottest day is this one. I blame
the thin shine of sweat on my bare arms

and the light black hair clouding my tattoos.
I am rusting out like a Ford
abandoned in brush off the fire road,

and I blame the mosquito I would slap
if I could kill anything, directly,
if I could answer a yes or no question

with anything but the least oblique
word my white stone struggles to conjure.
You ask, if we were teleported to a quiet

room far from trees at their present height
and the Housatonic at its current depth,
would you grow a shade garden

under my tallest interior maples?
Recklessly says my spade, my shovel,
the sparkling loam I turn over.

Dusk is the Light I Want You

At the midpoint between
your barn and my garage,
a public commuter lot of infallible

discretion, we meet: Skull
and Roses Duo, make-believe
criminals, Black Bird Society.

Terrible dusk sneaks between
My motorcycle and your truck.
Number each deep breath, each

casual profanity when the patrol car
rolls by in acknowledgment. Even
the growing oil spots between

lines lie complicit. *Restriction*
is the latest small word, no
bigger than a barn swallow,

no smaller than a rust particle
on the self-tapping screw I drove
into my motorcycle's frame last

night, to fasten a brake switch,
so I could fake *street legal*,
as though there were any possibility

of stopping my machine, too sleek
and gleaming. Pavement is fine,
or the dirt arena where you lunge

your horse, but we prefer pines
composing an advancing hillside.
If I drive you behind that veil,

if I can even see the road through
this fever, promise me land-
scape over abstraction, quagmire

over quandary, messy state
the lot takes as my aching feet
are sinking, near sunk, beside yours.

We peer into the tinted windows
of some goner's teal and dented
Dodge Neon and make out a leopard-

print bra draped over the passenger
seat, a huge soda cup brimming
with cigarette butts, and just above

the steering wheel, a head-size
spiderweb crack in the windshield.
Nowhere is a thing worth stealing.

Instead, I have in my knuckle a hot
metal sliver I will let you pick out
with your teeth if you promise

to keep it forever and clean up
any blood you leave. Then share
your cold coffee, never enough

at sundown, the only light I want
to look directly into, our slipping
vantage point, even deeper breath.

Dusk is the light I want you
to stretch my once-broken back
under, or if we leave in your truck,

the ray I want to bend around
the corner of your red barn until
all orange slips into the jagged

black hillside, my hand snuck
into your jeans' back pocket, spit
concealed in sweat, saved

for later, because *later* is all
we have, all we'll know, if we keep
hiding every skull we've collected:

polaroids, anatomical clip art,
tattoos: and even though skulls
eat roses, if we hold each inky

crow and its branch only half visible
(up my sleeve, above your hip)
then *later* will remain an ache

under your sternum I cannot
thumb out, one more feeling of *never*,
expansive dark over the only

road in the Valley that leads to sweat
soaking my thinnest t-shirt, a shiny bow
of teeth marks on my shoulder.

Jackie in the Eye of a Black Bear

There was a bear
in my woods last night
I can't prove it

What I choose
to believe is
a rangy smell in the leaves

a giant paw's impression
pungence of a certain declension
One bear roaming

a small area brings
a dozen supposed sightings
the neighborhood's burden

Fear is breathing
at a delayed interval
fright is

at the back door
Despite what the evening
news may say

ammonia in the trash
and keeping meat out of the compost
won't save you

Map of the Emerald Ash Borer

You stuff your day with carbohydrates
and never cardio them away
It stopped raining so you could
water your neon envy of the neighborhood
You lean increasingly to the right
then to the left and it is like walking
You push the mower in such straight rows
but you're no *weedwacker* who sleeps in a truck
Your buzzing pocket is filling up
with pics of last night's right swipe
and some satanic insect is hollowing out
the hundred-year-old ash
Hide your filthiest flash drive
in the sawdust pooling around the base
so the tree leans toward the street
and the telephone poles tip
increasingly toward your property
The land line's dial tone is all feedback
and the digital cable delivers two hundred
channels of a standby message
The service lady says *solar flares*
but she's conspiring against the poor
on behalf of the rich or vice versa
You are full full full of contempt
for both the World Protest Channel
and the National Restoration Network
Your freakout is best expressed in explicit

texts of cute typos and obsolete slang
so you spoonfeed your temper the lukewarm
rest of the less of the less of the less
until the birdbath is just slime
barely reflecting a single engine cliché
nose diving out of a breaking cloud

Lake for Jackie

If looming grey threatens to soak
another Monday and the bewilderment
between us is running pink, can that thin noise
coax you from your bright white apartment
of pathological nitpickery and into my filthy
truck of drive first and think later? Literally,
the road has to end in trees, and it does.
We make time for three laps around the reservoir.
Wet pine needles underfoot will pad our steps.
I want to listen to your stories of fleeing
to Taos, the drummer in leather pants
who brought you to an overlook to break
your heart, the dark week you had nowhere
to sleep. On the way play me voluminous

cassette tapes of you reading
from your old journals, even if it takes the whole
drive to reach the passage describing a hospital
scene I'll misinterpret as *bodies*
negotiating physical space. We must encode
the true subject: There are names
written all over you, there are names
you can't remember, there were costumes
and there were lies. I will listen and listen
with discipline, my quiet, and my face
will not strangely ache when I am driving
home to my wife's worry at 2 a.m.

Blue breaks the cloud cover, briefly, and lights
your cell photo of new grey in my beard,

ledge and pine and cloud in the water.
Cold and mist are the light of a man made
lake that stands not for the advance of the sea,
but for pages cut from a book that draws
connections between ancient oceanic realms
and modern hypnosis, a strained relationship
which stands for some tremendous despair.
On the other side is light on a locked barn
full of vintage postcards from golden beaches,
lovers on the backs smudged in blue: *goodbye*.
Light is green on the rocks and brown
in the weeds. I don't think it's only the cold
when your cheeks go pink and we attempt
to list everything that the light isn't.

Jealousy

It's not that we don't want to be seen,
or the cautious way I lift a bite
to your mouth the second all attention

in the restaurant turns to sirens
out the window. It's not the slender shape
of the three-pronged fork, its weight

on your lip, the metal warm
and still tasting of my mouth.
The chic peas in chili pepper do not cause

this weird burn, like anger but not anger
deepening under the sternum, the lick
no amount of adoration can smother.

You believe this act, me feeding you,
is so yours that your desire alone
is what draws my hand up. Dusk is burning

not because another once asked for me
to feed her; what you can't bear is that
I stayed when she was no longer hungry.

The future, you and me not having one another—
my pain, my Valley, once thrived in the abstract.
But now I can unimagine the lanky man,

~~the inches he has over me, the sinewy arms~~
~~lifting your baby toward morning light.~~
~~I erase that invention: nothing.~~ Today

I am blinded by the actual, the experiments
of the past, a shorter man's sleeping bag
unzipped so many times it bred your prowess:

the way your spidery fingers can dig old hurt
from muscles, the way you pitch
your length and hips and obliterate reason,

the pressure of your slightly crooked teeth
and their measured impression. It's not that
you have wanted someone. It's the terrible fact

that you have been wanted, that he came
again and again for you, that he can still
conjure your deepest breath in his sleeping bag.

Consolation for Jackie

Later in the landscape, a week
of unmemorable weather,
I regretted never donating

a yellow object
to your *community project*:
a distorted recording

of original chamber music, a grid
of blurry Polaroids, a swatch
of sod cut from every third lawn.

Nobody could explain
the unifying concept
in your collage.

Under a lemon with a cartoon face
wandering the night sky,
a yellow convertible swerved

to avoid a giant corn cob pipe.
Seldom does a driver expect the road
to be that slick. But inside,

the dimmers down, the desk lamp off,
my stack of pristine magazines
tipped toward fresh anxieties.

These days my story, just ducks
landing on the Housatonic at dusk,
is hardly worth your camera. No truck

crashing and sinking. The lack of yellow
stalls as negative space—taken off,
a tire, a rind, a ring fills with light.

Call any previous uncertainty
by its rightful name:
Resentful Weather Swiftly

East Above Stop-and-Go
on the Crumbling Interstate.
All bets are off.

Out-of-body in the skyscape,
attention in cirrus clouds, I looked
down on a mountain

of mostly green and rejected
the idea of a search party, another
exaggeration of urgency lacking

prescience as to which place, plant,
or body a yellow object
might turn up next.

The cloud at my back pushes
toward the salvage yard on the hill,
the electric fence that protects us

from the wreck. I have to keep walking
up, up into branches resembling neurons
in black and white. I'll see it first.

New Haven on the eastern horizon
distorts from this angle, this
altitude. I swear

to never again mention our lament,
slow to fade, still grey and darkening—
It offers no new yellow.

Map into (White Trees at the Edge of) Possible Valley

days of rain project
ennui in morning
can't *explain to me*
mist and grey I project

into lowest June's
Possible Valley
fog and wood smoke
vivid heaps of white

leaves give the far side
of these eighteen acres
a black horse grazing
in drizzle and dim light

white leaf is like a moth
wing I'd fix to her shoulder
what breath is absent
from the air and the dust

Map of Broken Glass

after Robert Smithson

We can't go back
to that city
of obsolete electronics

and broken guitar strings,
a country
too actual.

Every other continent
is a fiction
we find permission

to frame:
a river,
no freeze almost factual.

Seldom do we fracture
a plot
we did not shape—

we say
I have lived there,
morning drizzle in traffic.

Years later
a chip of windshield surfaced
below my elbow.

I have since lost it,
though not the lens
or the spot of blood.

I would have saved
every tiny reflection
picked out

with surgical tweezers,
gauze pads dabbed
with alcohol.

But there are safer
ways of sleep-driving
than listening

for the turkey vulture
trailing
in your blind spot.

We have lived there,
in the crime
of ornament,

the artificial
leaf that distracted us
from burning

city lights
into photo paper,
as a lack of money

precludes building a box
of window walls
into a granite

outcropping.
No architect could devise
a site of constraints

superior
to a jagged slope,
edge of dark woods.

The window
into which
the gold finch crashes

and the twitch
are both
a fiction.

The decision
to move on
is not the decision

not to stay.
That the glass
becomes fragile

with the chill
is a fiction
and doesn't exactly

matter to you
who attracts the small
and the hungry.

A shattered windshield,
one kind of edge—
blue-green,

abstract, it refracts
all recollection.
The edge of dusk

is a branch reaching
into a photo taken tomorrow.
The vessel I work

to slow
glints as it goes
and comes up

one miniscule chip
short/shy
of the pasture

in the valley
where fog collects
around a horse's legs.

If forgetting
were easy would we
desire it

like blue shapes frozen
between
oak branches.

The December tree
isn't the sketch
but it is

the plan. I can name
no city where
you don't enter

on an angle,
no county
of only circles,

and nowhere
that lacks the steely rain,
the muted glare.

I have lived
in negative space,
the deserted

city of no beloved,
no in-between, no ghost
of burning oak.

What can we do but loathe
the smoke of it,
the lung of a true love

blackening.
Jackie keeps my window
unlocked

because the door
would wake me
under morning stars.

There are worse
scenarios
than the promise of return.

Postcards from the Periphery

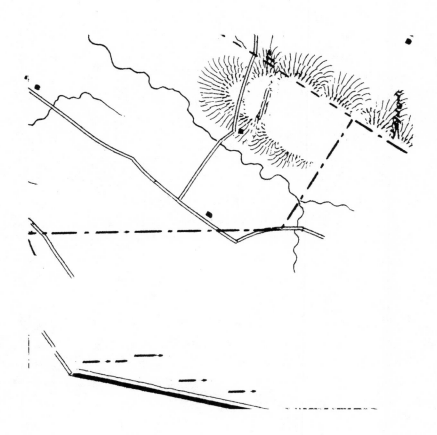

Skyscape Tattoo

When the light scab peeled the color
was not so bright, but right.
It took a week. I drove down the coast.
I flaked over the eastern states
and shed ashy skin in the ocean
not to find a beach that resembles yours
but to be the cold current
that holds you. My masochism
is not a diving dragon nor my vanity
a floating swan.
My blackbird glides by a twisting
branch and the simultaneous
seasons of three leaves:
all green, yellow edges, brown dust.
You have to imagine the tiny
black pebble settled in the bird's belly.
The pebble stands for the difference
between night and dark, between
sound sleep and ceaseless car alarms
in a city that couldn't have you.
Open skin tone around the wings
depicts not air but a warm glow
I hesitate to call negative space.
You have to imagine a ghost.
Fleas live hidden in its feathers.
A fine outline contains a determined
eye, its miniscule pupil shining.

No window frames your blue gaze
rippling—always toward the sea.
My browns wander block after block
of row homes and bodegas, none blue,
for your slight frame and brown braid,
the diminished possibility.
I would push up my sleeve to show you
the severe point of this beak.
It would take a week of walking
closely around this northern city, close
to water yet far from the sea.
This land bird bears your name
in the way only a rooftop view can explain:
deep sheen of tailfeathers over
the park where none of the young
girls reading under the trees can swim.

Map Tearing Inside a Tornado

My sleepless ice dwindles
into the warming arctic, my every
bit of plastic particulate swirls
in the North Pacific, my gulf's green
suffocates on the dark-slicked banks—
A power line whips the sidewalk
but the images stay up on my screen
shaking so much it's going to shatter.
The devices stop communicating.
A muscle car calendar scatters from a patio
and the pages catch in the maple
with the wail of the sirens.
The thinnest diseased limb snags me,
I won't decompose.
The flash flood through the side yard
is white noise at my knees,
I will go on to poison even stardust.
I am one hundred ninety pounds
of preservatives, antibiotics, and caffeine
rain-soaked and panicking for shelter.
I was too late to board the doors, I forget
the warning and press my chest
against both sides of the picture window.
My last locatable belief was in the shift
from weird grey to the lightness
of a pickup truck, now all I know is
I would bury this berserk wind

and collect the neon Chemlawn clippings
blowing through the blown out
cellar window, my next spring
gone well before the first snow—
My affinity for unseasonable weather
cools. I collect and count the wet blades
and strip away the pesticides
with my teeth. O my polar ice cap
creeping toward a lower river, O
my crowning ozone a hundred tons
of satellite wreckage crashes through,
O my beloved house whose roof
ripped clean off takes out the pages
but not the siren in the maple.
My roof takes off the top of the maple.

After Leadbelly

Moaning is the minute
between dusk
and dark, the first
stars, barely a breeze,
a dead armadillo in the road,
the day's cotton
picked, a blood-blistered
finger, a blind singer
led across Texas by thirst,
one side of the bed
still empty, a silhouette
slipping out the back door
as blue goes black

Ground Floor Music Room

I locked the door with a password impossible
to remember. I forgot
the floor plan if there ever was one.
I estranged the people by way of their pictures
and a stubborn bandmate lingered.
When I said *mess* I meant *miss*.
I cast off a hundred method books
that couldn't live up to their titles, then compiled
a list: *throw out the tattered scores,*
donate the stopped metronome, clear
and dismantle the makeshift table strewn
with blue bottles and brass bells, a microtonal range.
I bagged my emphatic wardrobe, boxed
the records categorically, scrapped
the obsolete electronics connected by a trap
of shorting cables. *Out with all instruments!*
For months I changed banjo strings
just to snap them and repeatedly dropped
a borrowed theremin. Kissed away
my embouchure and smoked away
my wind. Nothing kept is nothing to fix.
Not the cracked headstock on Jackie's abandoned
mandolin, not the deflated armchair/floatation
device, not my bad eye/ear for kitsch.
When I said *hostage* I meant *storage*,
or vice versa. Now the walls are clean and white
and the floor clear, save a square rag rug

to tighten the acoustics. The sun shines in.
This room will never be empty with two windows
open to the street, the perfect stereo field.

The Atheist's Piano

A small brown body slumped
against a wall
is just a clump of wet leaves. Light

changes from rain to heat wave, clouds
gathering over the skyline and burning off.
Bodies fly through this.

A flash in a bare branch or barred window
obscures the sound of airplanes,
but one's belief goes on, only

somewhere else, left behind
like directions scrawled in black marker
on the back of a diner placemat

the first rainy night I drove to Queens
to listen to you play. I am allowed
my past in that apartment, at least

my version of it, the radiator steam
that continues to disperse
and will, eventually, burn off

of so much else. The arguments
in young Spanish that came through
the wall are, by now,

only a stranger's vague resentment
that lingers like the ache in my neck
because I could never stop tracking jets

descending over the island.
Always up to pitch, the piano in the corner.
The proselytizing tuner would never admit

that the blemishes—the cigarette burn,
a ring from a sweating bottle—were the reason
your upright boomed like a grand.

A rationalist and a ray of light sit at a bar.
The rationalist says to the ray of light,
I can't go on like this.

The ray of light's reply is so blinding
that everyone leaves
their half-empty glasses and disappears

into the street. One holy land
abandoned for the promise of another.
I'm going to line my tires with money.

The day the air goes out and the sky
opens with lightning and dark rain, I will
spend it all on you if you let me

tell you, now five years and two boroughs later,
my recurring dream where we ride
the subway over a new and freezing

bridge. I ask to warm my hands
in your giant fur hat, I put in my left earbud
and give you the right, then

everything goes black. The instant
our train crosses from tunnel blackness
into nightlight, music comes to us.

In the smallest apartment in the most dangerous city,

any shots unheard
we dreamed,
and those neither

actual nor imagined
came from stolen guns,
ones with silencers.

Boredom and humidity,
the center
of every evil.

The ceiling fan
whirred,
Jackie stirred.

Slow,
I peeled the sheets
from her thigh.

The Truth About Hartford

If I were a touch taller,
if I were braver and
never so splayed on the daybed,

if we killed the side of me
that is part secrecy and part
confusion, could we

chart the undetectable
and quivering dimension called
Lower Sky.

Nobody has the heart
to tell you
my illustration of string theory

is not quite improvised,
that I traced Hartford in the atlas
with a gel pen—

I can neither find my keys
nor explain
the subatomic world to you.

Lies about Hartford abound.
But my drawing demonstrates
Stevens lived nowhere but

Lower Sky, as did Twain,
though he was a bit more Buffalo,
a tad Tennessee.

Nobody else can bear
to drive you around impoverished
neighborhoods where

the air right above the sunroof
feels just like what blows in
through the windows.

If east-bound began with our heads down
to follow the black lines, it ends
in disappointment—

countless vacancies, dark
windows welcoming no one.
The small questions

add up to something hazy
and unnamed, the body's rising
intonation, wanting to thrive

in every empty office and storefront
at once. Stowe never arrives.
Here we are sounds different

than you'd expect, deflated,
and seems to say *it was naïve
to want downtown to bustle at sundown.*

If I were younger and airy
we might hover
over the capitol's glimmering dome.

Lost in Cedar Hill Cemetery
it doesn't help
to impersonate each other

and misquote ad nauseum
from *Harmonium*.
Jackie, if our connection is

borrowing one another's intonation,
whose ghost translates us, or
is our image doomed to caricature.

Where is the *physical* voice,
if not in the variable speed of wind,
the fixed speed of light, or

the meaningless black curve
that mimics imperfectly the interstate
in red, our heart of particles.

Postcards from the Periphery

That vintage beach
has its golden eye on you,
that sunset is full of ridicule.

But there is nothing to interpret
on the Shore of the Periphery, black and white
one day, color another—

She writes illegibly, she writes
nothing, it's printed and in cursive,
neither pen nor pencil.

*

The subject of the postcard
is Horizon, the subject
is History. The abstractions

where family and weather intersect.
The gradations of grey suggesting
shadow suggesting color

drive home your limits, the drama
mocks you from just beyond
your boundaries—a hologram,

you hang it between a toilet
full of Comet and every exotic fringe
she will not permit you.

You hang it on the fridge
with a magnet shaped like a tornado,
you tape it to the window, visible

from every room in which you shift
your weight from one foot to the other.
One foot to the other.

*

It keeps you safe.
If you tried to crease it
your arm would fracture,

if you tried to tear it
your heart would break.
Hold a match to it

and it will not catch.
In black marker
scribble out the shore,

and the shore will appear
a desert before returning
to a beach. Her message listens

to you sleep, her message
is mist over a wave
you can neither decipher nor erase.

*

What souvenir birds
she does not bring from
Pigeon Point, Praia do Sancho, Bottom Bay.

You strain to follow
the artificial light
neither gull nor vulture

shines down. Which is
circling
above your house.

*

Jackie traveled time and space
and all I got
was this crummy t-shirt.

Wear it till the neck frays
and the pink palm tree
flakes away.

It takes a willing figure
to intersect
the daunting line

drawn between land and sky—
Be the distant silhouette
that suggests

the shifting of the light.
You were almost
airbrushed out.

Dusk, Dog Pack, The Devil's Music

The road we named Moon Strip runs the ridge
of these out-of-bounds mountains

The sun sets between two blue hills
we named after nobody (out loud

You thought the temperature would drop
if we parked at this elevation

You can turn the radio on (please don't
You can turn the volume up (please do

The road's owned by domestic breeds
abandoned at the edge of the forest

That is not static (we're below the radio tower
I know the red light is blinking (beating beating

Keep the windows down
The dogs won't come if they can't smell us

The dogs won't come if they hear us
not talking (breathing breathing

You thought the temperature would drop
as everything blue grew black

All night the red light will keep flashing
Those are perfect harsh guitars

You can turn the volume up (please do
The dogs won't come if they can't hear us

It could be hours
before their haunting light-shocked eyes

The rough timbre and low pitch come
not from the singer's throat but the hour

I do not know this song (I revel
I do not know this song (I revel

Read to Me

From the note you wrote yourself
on your left wrist
and the word unwritten on your right

From the couch dragged off
the porch into the blue back yard

From the thrumming
aerospace factory
black and white you can't imagine

From the middle of the road
in the middle of the night

From the first three pages of coffee stains
in the dictionary you secretly carry

From the tattered price tag
kept in the pocket of your stolen jacket

From boulder-field lichens at sunset
not a jade blaze but slow
smoldering

From a motel room overlooking
rain in a distant city

From so many starlings
perforating a cumulonimbus crawling
orange into pink

From the clear
double exposure

a green mountain panorama over
a portrait of this garrulous man

X in the Orchard

She named no roads.

X was the common variable, in that case
uncommon initial that stood
for her unknown name.
I'm Sandra but call me Joanne no call me Jackie.
We picked at Vietnamese in silence
and I glimpsed the unmistakable X into a scribble
next to the X on the credit slip.
We joked in whispers through two movies:
the first flashed a string of crash scenes, the other
was more equestrian. *A white horse fell in the mud.*
She asked to stay the night
and sleep-talked into Sunday:
The route through the orchard is no escape.

She drifted out around dawn.

No evidence of X by the water but the water,
its advance and withdrawal.
No swimmers drag out remains
of the shipwreck she dreamed.
We were swimming for the life boat,
the water was burning.
Cannot count her among the horizon's
dumb audience dozing under so many umbrellas.
Like a field of stalled pinwheels, no sign

of any missing letter. The tide goes out.
The horizon is more a seam than a line.
The horizon points in two directions.

To choose one is to travel the other.

To reach the desert X didn't mean to mention
you must drive days through cornfields.
It is/isn't worth countless hours
of static and left-arm sunburn
to find so much hot rock and sand.
There are scorpions! Thieves who remember
nothing of X peddle hallucinogens
that fall short of the suburban legends.
The midnight sky never suggests a letter
you can remember—no matter how far and long
it travels, despite its perfect speed, light
would have to carry a message to be obsolete.

The midnight sky is nothing to blur.

Here is the city where the man who didn't name X,
who was/wasn't someone else's father,
lived and died in his car. In the salvage yard
a hubcap and a puddle go on
reflecting each other and the moon.
This is a feral cat, not a letter, not a clue.
According to my nightwatch
every lease on the block is up, the brass mill
burned, and soon comes another Sunday.

X is nowhere I wish to be.
I dread most the orchard between
this city and my own, the acres of shade.
I will walk beyond
the outskirts to return home, the margin,
not with a name, but smelling of apples.

American Aerospace

The summer I left for the desert
to become a UFO watcher
I set up camp behind a famous skull-
shaped boulder so big it blocked
my skyview, my faulty antenna, my hope
for the future of American Aerospace.
Then I got a deal on the new Electromagnetic
Center, cheap real estate, the plot
of sand and bramble most conducive
to time travel and cellular rejuvenation.
There, over scorching decades, I built
a wood dome of perfect acoustics.
Not the famous one, but a perfect replica.
Families from all over would arrive
at dawn in SUV's or hybrids and stay up
long past nightfall. They'd gaze up
until their foreheads sunburned
and their necks grew sore, but they never
saw anything strange fly over, no blue beam
reach down for their cooing/whining baby,
no big black eyes peer from behind a cactus.
So the travelers dodged the natives circling
on ATV's and came inside
my wood dome of perfect acoustics,
and despite my humble request for quiet,
the travelers bathed in the reverberation
of their own talking: golf, afterschool

activities, mutual funds. *Sigh.*
I chimed my imitation crystal singing bowls
for the last time and abandoned my dome
to scour the sand for transmitter-receivers—
bottle caps, lengths of rusting
barbed wire, bent bicycle rims—
any scrap of metal that could carry
to the future alien race my SOS:
The Electromagnetic Center has grown
crowded and weak with tourism.
Please send—

Easy Rider

I am unfolding
America's map again
I lean back

I lean forward
over the bars into nothing
that could support

even the lightest man
but I wasn't
born to follow

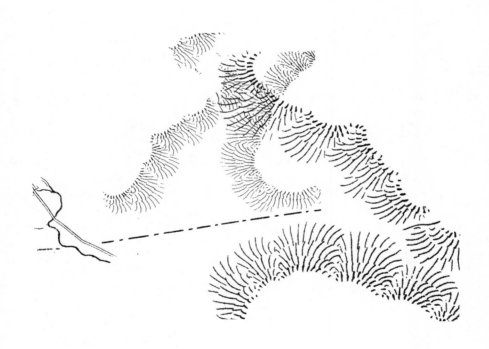

Acknowledgements

Thank you to the editors of the following publications, where some of these poems first appeared, often in different versions or with alternate titles: *Absent*, *AGNI*, *American Letters & Commentary*, *Conjunctions*, *DIAGRAM*, *Ephemeroptera*, *Everyday Genius*, *Gulf Coast*, *Indiana Review*, *Missouri Review*, *Quarterly West*, *Vanitas*, *Verse*, *Washington Square*, and *What Rough Beast*.

Boundless love and gratitude to all of my friends, family, and fellow musicians, without whom this would not be. Thank you to Geoffrey Gatza, Peter Gizzi, Melissa Labbe, Ann Lauterbach, Michael Palmer, and, especially, Melanie Willhide.

A note on the art: The interior images were created specifically for this book by artist Melanie Willhide, who made collages from a map of Bethany, Connecticut (1868) and a map of Virginia (1960's), two geographies important to this work. melaniewillhide.com

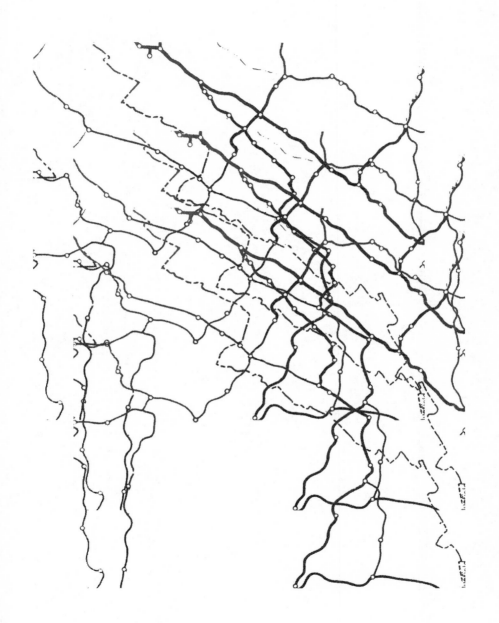

Jason Labbe's first book of poems, *Spleen Elegy*, came out in 2017. His work has appeared in *Poetry*, *Conjunctions*, *Denver Quarterly*, *Boston Review*, *A Public Space*, *The Brooklyn Rail*, and several chapbooks. He is a musician and divides his nights between Bethany, Connecticut and Brooklyn, New York.

Made in the USA
San Bernardino, CA
22 February 2020